Create Peace in Your Life Through Growth & Self-Development

By

Carrie Porter

This book is dedicated to:

My Sun's Colin and Caleb.

Table of Contents

Introduction

When I decided to write this book, my intentions were to share my views and perspectives on how I created peace in my life through growth and self-development. The first step in this process was identifying what brought me to this point in life. I needed to identify the steps that I took.

I would be lying if I told you it was easy, and that each of you reading this book will have the steps outlined on a silver platter. Life just does not work like that. Each day brings new challenges and new experiences that varies for each person, and we must learn to adapt to them. How you adapt makes all the difference. What I will say is that I have discovered in my personal experiences that if you choose to grow and develop in the six areas I will be discussing in this book, you will have the opportunity to create a life that is truly peaceful.

What is peace? What does it mean to be at peace? The definition of peace is "freedom from disturbance; tranquility." When I think of situations and circumstances that can disrupt one's inner peace, some of the thoughts that come to my mind include:

-Fear

-Anxiety

-Insecurities

-Negative Relationships (Personal/Work)

-Negative Environments

-Financial Concerns

-Lack of Discipline

-Instability

-Resentment

-Anger

-Bitterness

-Ineffective Communication

I refer to the above factors as *Peace Disruptors*. Take a moment and think about each one. Is there one or two that stands out to you personally? Are you allowing fear to stop you from pursuing your goals? Are you allowing insecurities to prevent you from loving all of you? Are your financial concerns wreaking havoc on you and your family? Are your poor communication skills creating more conflict in your life? If you can identify with any of these *Peace Disruptors*, you are not alone so stop being hard on yourself.

Here is a quick snapshot of my life. I was a teen Mom. I gave birth to my oldest son Colin when I was 16 years old. I played high school basketball and women's college basketball on scholarship. Two months after graduating from college with my Bachelor's Degree in Business Administration, I was pregnant with my second son. I gave birth to my youngest son Caleb the following year, which made me a mother of 2 by the age of 23. I started my career in Retail Management right after graduating. By the age of 29 years old, I completed my Master's Degree in Management. At 32 years old, I moved across the country from Chicago to Texas as a single parent. I have been with the same company for 14 years now. I have run from love quite a few times in life, made some not so good decisions, and I am still optimistic in everything that I do.

That was a pretty cluttered snapshot, right? I hope that it was because that is a snapshot of how life is. There are constant changes, circumstances, and challenges that can send our lives in various directions. How you adapt and respond to those changes will determine how peaceful your life can still be maintained. I live a peaceful life considering everything that I have been through in my young 38 years on this physical plane. I grew up too fast, I have had to make adult decisions as a teen, and I continue to learn as much as possible from my experiences (good and bad) as each day passes.

I have focused on six areas of self-improvement over the last few years that I wanted to grow and develop. I knew that if I could identify areas I needed to grow in, ultimately, I would become the best version of Carrie. I realized it all started with me, it started from within. I chose to be in control of my life. I chose to face my fears, anxieties, and insecurities head on.

The six areas I chose to focus on were:

-Self-Care

-Self-Love

-Self-Accountability

-Effective Communication

-Preparation

-Gratitude

These six areas of focus helped me to create a peaceful life. I am not the same person I was 10 years ago, 5 years ago, or 1 year ago because I am continuously learning and growing.

I am self-checking and always identifying areas I can improve on. *Self-Care* allows me to focus on what makes me feel good and brings happiness into my life. *Self-Love* allows me to build my confidence and aids in better decision making because I know what I deserve. *Self-Accountability* allows me to continue growing and maturing through situations. *Effective Communication* allows me to have better relationships and interactions. I have reduced conflict in my life to a bare minimum at work and at home. *Preparation* has allowed me to accomplish my goals at a faster rate and manage my finances better. Walking in *Gratitude* has continuously helped me maintain happiness, appreciation, and ultimate peace in my life.

Overall, I am happy that you decided to read my book. Let me be clear, peace does not mean that life is perfect all the time. We will continuously face challenges, need to adapt to change, and sometimes face unfortunate circumstances. That is life.

Peace in my eyes revolves around how you maneuver through those challenges. Focus on growing through your situations. Learn from your experiences. Keep your heart open and pure and allow peace in. I do not have all the answers. I will say that I am always open to learning and viewing life from various perspectives. I believe that by focusing on these six areas of growth and development, you will be able to handle any situations you encounter with a positive mindset that is solution based and will allow you to maintain continued peace throughout your journey.

Chapter 1:
Self-Care

"Take Care of Yourself, Love Yourself, Smile More, Feel Good More, Enjoy Life More."

~Carrie P.~

Chapter 1: Self-Care

Self-Care can directly affect how peaceful you are in life. Let's face it, life brings us so many challenges and obstacles that may affect our peace, joy, and overall happiness. During these difficult times in particular, we are battling COVID, rise in unemployment, loss of lives, and trying to adjust to our "new normal". Due to these unfortunate circumstances its more important now than ever to be in control of your mental clarity, have healthy and positive interactions, and focusing on your overall happiness. We still have children to raise, employees to mentor, family members to be there for, and a beautiful life to live. While it is not always easy, I try to be as happy as I can more often than others so that I can spread joy to as many people as possible during my daily interactions. Your happiness is the biggest expression of Self-Care. I am going to share with you some ways you can increase your happiness by indulging in activities of Self-Care.

A *healthy* person is a happy person. Creating a healthy lifestyle filled with exercise, activities, and getting out in nature will increase your happiness. Some activities you can indulge in includes yoga, hiking, fitness, walking, bike riding, dance classes, etc. The more active you are, the better your health will be. Not only should your focus be on physical activities, but you should make your diet a priority as well. When you eat better, you feel better. Taking in nutritional foods like more fruits and veggies will increase your energy as well as decrease your chances of becoming ill or developing ailments that will create suffering in your life. By making your health a priority you will ultimately become a happier person more often.

I am a firm believer that *meditation* creates more happiness in one's life as well. Meditating is a significant part of my life and aids me in dealing with challenging situations in a calming manner. Meditation builds your patience, appreciation for life, mental clarity, and allows you to understand various perspectives, and builds your mental strength. You can choose to meditate for 10 minutes a day or 1 hour a day. You can choose to meditate sitting down or laying down. Whatever your preference is, it is totally up to you. If you take time to meditate, clear your thoughts, silence your mind, and focus on growth and understanding, you will be able to deal with life situations much better. You will also gain more patience and ultimately create a happier aura daily.

I find that when I am taking on too much and lacking *rest,* I begin to feel overwhelmed which affects how happy I am each day. In some instances, motivation and determination drives us in a way that shifts our focus on tasks completion. We want to reach our goals at all cost. We live in a society that taught us that hard work pays off, so in some instances we work so hard that it negatively affects our appreciation for the journey. It affects our overall happiness with the success that we are striving for. I am guilty of this, which is why I am working on my work/life balance at this present time in my life. I make a conscious effort to get proper rest now. I search for activities that are relaxing on my off days because I understand that balance is important. I have found over the last few weeks that I have been happier when I am well rested. I recommend that you make rest and relaxation a priority in your life and in a short period of time you will see your daily doses of happiness increasing.

One of the fastest ways you can become more happier is to *do what you love doing*. You want to indulge in activities that make you happy. If you enjoy fishing, make time to go fishing once a week. If playing your favorite sport or enjoying spa days makes you happy, indulge. If you are a true gym rat or love painting, complete these activities regularly. Do not make excuses for not having time because that will decrease your happiness and joy. Find time in your schedule and make it happen. It is a known fact that the more time you spend doing things you love and enjoy, the happier you will be!

I found being out in nature to be my most loved Self-Care expression. I developed my love for nature when I moved to Texas in 2013. I am originally from Chicago where the land is flat, there are tall buildings everywhere, it is busy, and you get to experience nature in nice weather between April-October. When I moved to Texas, I loved feeling closer to the sun, seeing so much green, trees everywhere, hills on the highways, and witnessing so much beautiful land. It took me a few more years, 2015 to be exact, to genuinely appreciate all the aspects of nature that would turn out to be healing for me.

Over the last few years, I have captured hundreds of images that are buried in my phone as I traveled throughout Texas. Sometimes my excitement shocked my peers as I would snap a shot of a bird or a beautiful stretch of scenery. Last year for my 38th birthday I bought a new camera and I have been capturing the most beautiful images of plants, flowers, animals, and the elements.

Nature aids us in balancing out our daily stresses. Whether we are busy at work, busy parenting, dealing with extra curriculum activities, or stressing over bills, life can be overwhelming at times. How often do we have time, or better yet, make time to get out in nature? If you have not made time to do so, I am here to tell you that nature will help balance out the rough days you have behind four walls at work, and the time you spend behind 4 doors in cars commuting to work.

The beauty outside alone will make you smile. The silence allows you to stand still and gather your thoughts. Breathe slowly for a minute, listen to the wind, the trees, and the flow of the water. It is truly a calming and peaceful experience.

Being out in nature gives you a certain level of appreciation for plants, animals, and the environment. When I am out walking, I enjoy watching the birds, squirrels, and bugs moving about. They make me realize how big the world is, how precious life is, and how grateful I am to have the ability to continue my journey. I realize that their circle of life is no different than ours. I recall one day visiting trinity river and I watched a family of turtles in the water. A little further down that river I observed a family of ducks, and I was able to snap an image of a bee pollinating on a sunflower.

A few years ago, I would not have been interested or found joy in these little moments in time, but it is truly pure joy in my spirit. I took a few minutes listening to the water flowing and felt a rush of energy through my body. I zoomed in on trees and imagined how old they were. I noticed that the type of leaves on trees varied, and patches of grass that were way to dry. The focus and attention to details in nature are good for your mental health because it fills you with gratitude and appreciation. The peaceful feelings are surreal at times.

Ask yourself what are some self-care activities that you enjoy. Then ask yourself, how often you indulge in those activities. What is preventing you from enjoying activities that will aid in better mental health for you?

I have created a self-care grid on page 17 that you can use to identify the *Peace Disruptors* in your life surrounding self-care. After you identify some *Peace Disruptors*, identify some self-care activities to counter those disruptors. Lastly, list the benefits you will receive from the activities you listed. This should help you focus more on how you can make self-care a daily routine in your life.

Self-Care is about you taking care of you without guilt. For you to be great in the world, you must be great to yourself first. You are a priority. You are special. You need to feel good. You should feel love. You deserve happiness. It is okay to spend time alone. You deserve pampering. You deserve to smile. The more time you spend indulging in self-care, the deeper you dive into Self-Love and creating peace in your life.

Create Peace In Your Life Through Growth & Self-Development

Peace Disruptors	*Self-Care Activity*	*Benefits of this Activity*
Work Overload	Meditate daily	Allows me to clear my mind and start my day on a positive note.
Too much emotional baggage	Write in my journal once a week	Allows me to express and release my thoughts, joys, concerns, and experiences.
Exhausted from stress	Go to the gym daily	Allows me to be healthy and relieve daily stressors.
Not feeling physically confident	Go to the Spa once a month	Allows me to be pampered and experience relaxation.
Frustrated/ Overwhelmed	Get out in nature at least 10min everyday	Allows me to enjoy the weather, sun, animals, and trees. Aids in my appreciation for life.

Self-Care Grid Example

Chapter 2: Self-Love

"Love All of You, Appreciate All of You, Expect More, Exude Confidence, Stand Tall."

~Carrie P.~

Chapter 2: Self-Love

Self-love is choosing you first. Self-love is not accepting treatment that you do not deserve. Self-love is holding yourself to a higher regard and standard that is filled with love, joy, and respect. Self-love is knowing that happiness, confidence, and self-appreciation comes from within. Self-love starts with you, not an outside source.

Self-love can come and go and come again based on a variety of factors throughout our lives. Some of those factors may include loss of a loved one, abusive relationships, self-esteem issues, traumatic childhood, or spending time in environments or around people that are over critical and negative towards you. Whatever reason or point in your life that you may have experienced a lack of self-love in, I am here to tell you that you are not alone...

Self-love is loving you for who you are, choosing to be happy, surrounding yourself with positive people, and engaging in environments that add peace and joy into your life. Self-love is knowing your worth, valuing your attributes, and not allowing others to treat you less than you deserve.

Create Peace In Your Life Through Growth & Self-Development

Self-love can deteriorate as you turn over your power and confidence to others. It decreases as your interactions in negative environments increase. It decreases as people who lack good intentions enter your life, and you accept treatment that is unkind. It decreases as you start viewing yourself through the lenses of others. As you compare yourself to others, you will most likely decrease the love of self. As days, months, or years go by, you may find yourself unhappy and lacking the most important ingredient to you experiencing a fruitful life: Self-Love.

There are various experiences or reasons why someone would begin to lack self-love. Failed relationships, mental, physical, or emotional abuse, weight loss or weight gain, lack of employment, body image perceptions, and insecurities could all lead to one decreasing self-love.

I have experienced many of these situations throughout my life. I make a conscious effort to focus on building self-love because I have realized that I am deserving of peace, joy, and happiness. I also understand that I am responsible for me loving myself unconditionally.

I believe there are four actions you can incorporate into your life to begin building self-love which also aids in creating peace in your life: ***Self Accountability, Letting Go of Fears and***

Regrets, Acknowledging Your Accomplishments, and Keeping High Spirits.

Hold Yourself Accountable For Your Life!

Once you realize that you are responsible for what and who you allow in your life, you shift the burden of blame away. Self-accountability helps you to make better decisions going forward. You make better judgement calls. You understand that no force outside of you can control you without your permission. Do not eat that extra piece of cake. Do not stay in that abusive relationship longer than you should. Do not wait for the green light to start that business.

Be in control of your life. The more control you have in your experiences the more self-love you will develop. I am not saying transitions will be easy, but you are responsible for making necessary adjustments that benefit you. Ultimately, you will be so much happier when you get comfortable with self-accountability and taking control of your happiness. We will talk more about this topic later in the book.

Let Go Of Fears And Regrets!

Fears and Regrets will deter you from loving yourself, so it is best to take steps to let them go. They will also deter you from internal peace. We have all had those moments when we felt we should have or could have done some things differently. Just remember, you cannot change what happened, you should focus on not making those same decisions going forward.

When living with regrets, you are displacing your energy and focus into the wrong direction. Shift your focus to the lessons and what you learned from those experiences. Holding on to fears are just as bad as holding on to regrets. Hanging on to fears will stop you from attempting a life that you deserve. You will never know what is behind the door if you are too afraid to open it.

Love yourself more for making it through those challenging times, and the fact that you can start a new experience at any time you choose. As you begin to let fears and regrets go, you will begin to have new experiences that will aid in an increase in peace in your life.

Acknowledge Your Accomplishments and Encourage Positive Self Talk!

You need to take time to give yourself credit for your accomplishments. Some people mistake self-love and self-confidence for arrogance. It is not arrogant for you to acknowledge your successes and celebrate your wins.

Create Peace In Your Life Through Growth & Self-Development

During the age of social media, it is more important now than ever to encourage and praise you for your greatness. Why not? Positive self-talk will ward off some of the negativity in your world. Why does it seem that we will acknowledge our flaws or focus on areas to improve on more than our assets, gifts, talents, and accomplishments? It is a thin line between being humble and not pumping yourself up with confidence and positive energy you deserve. I used to be too humble, and now I make a conscious effort to tell myself when I am doing a good job, look in the mirror and admire my beauty while embracing my flaws, and encouraging myself to be confident.

My self-love, values, and standards match how I am beginning to feel about myself now. I encourage you to monitor your self-talk and make sure you are leaning more on the positive side and less on the self-critical side of the spectrum.

For as long as I can remember, I was always striving for the idea of perfection. I am not just referring to physical appearance, but how I am being perceived from my actions and my words as well. Some of the biggest decisions and leaps of faith I pursued in life were sometimes delayed. The delays were mainly due to me believing it had to be the "perfect" time and I was not 100% prepared. Little did I know there would be circumstances that would occur that would push me over the ledge so that I had no choice but to FLY...

I realized in my early 30's that there is no perfect time to create the experiences you desire to have in life. My perception was flawed because I was too focused on people's perception, what others believed my timeline should look like, and what society's standards of beauty were. I had to go inside and reinforce my *self-love* so that my perception held the top ranking.

In those moments when you are in your head critiquing, feeling overwhelmed, bubbling up insecurities, and pointing out your flaws just remember that there is *only 1 you*, and you are *special*.

Whether you want to write a book, or become a dancer, learn to play the piano, or become a body builder you have the potential to do so. If you are reading this book, then your timeline is still shifting, and you have the choice to create the experiences you desire. Give yourself more credit for how far you have come and keep expanding. Tune into mediums that motivate and inspire you and view your life through your two eyes with optimism.

Stay In Good Spirits! Keep Happy Vibrations Flowing!

Create Peace In Your Life Through Growth & Self-Development

I cannot stress this action enough folks. It is imperative that you keep your vibrations high! You want to interact with people who have positive intentions. It is best that you spend time in environments that feel good for your spirit, that feels good for your soul.

Make your health a priority because when you feel good physically, you will feel good emotionally and mentally. Eat healthy foods because good nutrition gives your body more energy. Watch movies, videos, and lectures that make you feel happy and encouraged. The more you know the more you grow, so never stop learning! As you learn, your vibrations and your confidence will rise. In the moments that you feel down and need a boost, listen to music that uplifts you and brings you joy.

If you can reach a high level of self-love you will minimize your chances of being in situations that negatively impacts the peace you have in your life.

I have created a Self-Love grid on the next page that will help you identify some Peace Disruptors you are currently experiencing in the areas of self-love. Take some time to be honest with yourself by grabbing a journal or sheet of blank paper and listing some reasons you are not loving yourself properly. They can include insecurities, fears, depression, etc. Then you want to list the main concerns. After identifying some main concerns, create an action plan on ways you can rid yourself of those *Peace Disruptors*. Remember that honesty is the best policy, and you are not alone.

Create Peace In Your Life Through Growth & Self-Development

<u>Self-Love Grid Example:</u>

Peace Disruptors	***Main Concerns***	***Action Plans***
Insecurities	**Weight**	**Create a workout plan**
Anxiety	**Public Speaking**	**Take a speaking class**
Fear	**Make bad decisions in choosing partners**	**Identify 10 top qualities you are looking for.** **Always discuss these top areas before committing.**

Chapter 3:
Self-Accountability

"Own Your Mistakes. Grow Through What You Go Through. Accept Yourself 100%."

~Carrie P.~

Chapter 3: Self-Accountability

Why is it that we find it easier to blame outside sources for negative experiences that we have had, and focus on how "they" made us feel? We focus on how "they" controlled that outcome or that situation. We focus on how mad, angry, and upset we are with "them".

We spend weeks, months, and sometimes years carrying buckets of painful emotions around with us hoping that outside person or source will make us feel better about the situation or experience. "They" should make the changes and help fix us.

What if I told you that a simple solution could help you begin the healing process? What if I told you that you can start the process of emptying that annoying bucket of pain by identifying your role in the situations, and why holding yourself accountable can assist you in mental freedom.

Self-Accountability Relieves You Of Regrets

I am sure we have all experienced some situations when we did not make the best decisions. We wanted a particular outcome to occur, and it did not happen. These situations can range from staying in an abusive relationship too long, staying with a company too long, moving across the country for love and the relationship not working out, etc., etc. I can go on, but I am sure you get the point.

When the situation was over, we felt a variety of emotions like anger, disappointment, regret, sadness, or even depression. We wished we could turn back the clock and start again, but it was not possible.

From my personal experiences in these types of situations, I have found that the more angry or disappointed I became with my decisions, the worst I felt. The more regrets I had, the deeper into negative emotions I fell. Through my experiences what gave me comfort and allowed me to feel better was self-accountability. When I began shifting my thought process from "blaming" myself and others, to owning my decisions and my role throughout the experience I began to let go of my regrets. It was easier to reflect on those situations and identify the lessons I needed to learn. I was able to smile knowing that my intentions were good, and that experience was just a part of my journey.

Self-Accountability Helps You Move On

If you genuinely want to move on from a broken heart or painful situation self-accountability will help you do so. Being stuck in the past never helped anyone, especially when you feel sadness or resentment as part of the memories. A lot of times we want an apology from a person, or we wanted that person to change, or we wanted that company to give us a raise or promotion. We wanted the other source to help us feel better. We subconsciously believed that if we get the relief from the source that made us feel bad, we can then move on.

Once you realize you need to forgive yourself and own your decisions, you would be able to not only move on, but move on faster.

Self-Accountability Allows You To Learn And Grow

An amazing benefit of self-accountability is that you gain the ability to learn and grow! If you do not hold yourself accountable there is a great chance you are going to miss out on many lessons. Not catching the lessons may lead to you recycling the same experiences and making the same decisions again.

For example, I remember early in my career, I was disappointed that I was not promoted. I worked overnight for 6 years because it was a great schedule for my family at the time. I completed my Master's Degree during those years and believed I would be promoted as soon as I had my Degree in hand. It turned out the person that was promoted had more hands-on experience. He was more knowledgeable about the job because he gained skills working during the day, that I did not while working overnight.

I was initially upset. Once I identified that working overnights were impacting my growth with this company, I adjusted my schedule. Instead of blaming the company, I took self-accountability and learned from the experience.

I make a conscious effort to look at situations from this same mindset. I will be honest, I am usually upset in the beginning of an uncomfortable situation, but after things have calmed down a bit, I tend to view the situation from a "Self-Accountability" perspective, and I continuously grow from each experience.

Self-Accountability Will Increase Your Confidence

When your focus on a situation is geared toward blame and regret, it is easier to feel insecure or diminish your character. You are asking yourself questions like: Why wasn't I good enough for him/her? Was I not good enough for that promotion? Why doesn't he/she respect me? Am I weak?

Questions like these are most likely stemming from lack of self-value. Remember that your self-worth and value begin within. By continuing to wonder what that source outside of you felt about you, you will ultimately feel worse. Start focusing on why you allowed that behavior/treatment and work on fixing it.

Switch your thought process and ask questions that will help you grow. Self-Accountability will help you to recognize that you made the decision, focus on building your confidence again, and affirm that you will not make those same decisions in the future.

I believe that it is easier to blame someone else for your decisions because it can be difficult to be honest with yourself at times. Looking at yourself in the mirror and owning your mistakes can be challenging. Through those challenges, I have found that self-accountability has helped me grow and get past traumatic situations so much faster.

Holding myself accountable has made me more conscious and aware of my decisions and has played an integral role in my overall evolution as a person. I have gained so much mental freedom by focusing on self-accountability during my encounters. I recommend focusing on self-accountability throughout your journey's and beginning the process of dumping that bucket of pain that is weighing you down to allow peace into your lives.

Chapter 4:

Effective Communication

"I Communicate With Clarity. I Listen. I am Open To Details. I Have A Plan."

~Carrie P.~

Chapter 4: Effective Communication

Without Communication, how would we navigate through the world? Not only is communication important, but **effective communication** is even more important. Whether we are communicating with our family members, employees, or our co-workers, how we communicate determines the outcome of that conversation. Our goal is usually to teach, mentor, lead, express a message, or explain something to someone. Ultimately, we want that message to be received. When communicating effectively we should keep in mind these 4 areas to focus on: *Listening, Body Language, Being Precise, and Being Open-Minded.*

Listen

Always keep in mind that communication is a two-way street. You should be willing to not only share your thoughts and point of views, but to also listen to what the other party has to say. Otherwise, the conversation will become one sided, and the other party may feel attacked.

For example, you want to have a conversation with an employee who needs to improve in some areas. You sit down with that employee, share your concerns, and end the conversation with a threat of accountability if they do not improve in those areas.

That was not effective communication because you did not ask questions and possibly offer solutions to assist this employee in improvement. You did not open the opportunity to receive their feedback or stance on what may be affecting their productivity.

This holds the same weight when communicating with your loved ones. You want to receive their perspectives and how they feel about the subject as well. Therefore, you want to make sure you are prepared to listen if you want an effective conversation with a positive outcome.

Body Language

You want to be sure you have the correct body language going into a conversation with someone if you want to have an effective conversation. Your posture, eye contact, facial expressions, your tone, and use of space can affect the outcome.

If you look upset, disappointed, are fidgeting, or looking down, this might make the other party uncomfortable or even feed off the same energy. You want them to feel calm and open to the conversation, so it is best to display that same type of energy.

Presenting a confident, relaxed, and calming body language can make the difference in the outcome of this communication.

Be Precise

Before attempting to communicate an issue or concern, take a minute or two to plan that conversation. Create an outline of approach so that you are clear and able to get your message across. You do not want to draw the conversation out too long or be scattered everywhere and forget what intention you originally had going in.

Narrow down the message you want to express and hit points. You do not want this communication to turn into a long argument or a debate, so you must control the direction of the communication. That will become challenging if you do not have a plan going in.

Know the behaviors and personality of the person you are going to communicate with. Everyone is different, so you be sure to plan your approach ahead of time and intend on being specific in the approach. Be precise in your communication for the best end results.

Be Open Minded

Finally, go into the conversation with an open mind. If you think that you can communicate effectively without being able to absorb other people perspectives and views, you are in for a rude awakening. It is a must that you have an open mind. It is important to control your emotions and leave the door open for various opinions and observations. Everyone will not always agree with your perspective so be sure to not take it personal.

We all have room for improvement and communicating effectively sometimes mean that your self-accountability can change that conversation drastically. I sometimes mention areas that I can improve on as well so that the other party feels I am coming from a genuine place of self-accountability and not from a place of judgement.

Overall, effective communication can change various outcomes at work or at home. What it looks like to me is two parties having a conversation, coming up with a solution, and leaving that conversation in a positive mindset. Effectively communicating will not always be easy, but it is worth the effort. Being able to communicate with sincerity, respect, and understanding will drastically decrease the amount of conflict you experience throughout life which leads to a greater amount of peace.

Chapter 5:

Preparation

"I Adapt To Change. I Prepare For Challenges. I Anticipate Continuous Growth."

~Carrie P.~

Chapter 5: Preparation

How prepared you are to tackle this thing we call life, will either set you up for success or set you up for failure. Preparation will create peace in your life or create a great amount of chaos. Some of the *Peace Disruptors* you may experience surrounding preparation may include:

-Anxiety leading up to a big presentation

-Worry and Stress over Lack of Finances

-Depression over physical appearance

-Anger over lack of promotion

-Regrets over not pursuing your dreams (Entrepreneurship, Living Abroad, Etc.)

Those were just a few circumstances that may disrupt peace in our lives, and I believe that goal setting can be a huge help in becoming not only better prepared for handling these types of situations, but also accomplishing the goals you desire.

If you have anxiety about an upcoming presentation, set a goal to practice each day for an hour. If you are worried about how you are going to pay a bill, research ways to earn extra money on the side or figure out ways to decrease some of your expenses. If you are regretting not pursuing your dreams, what is stopping you from creating a business plan?

What I am trying to say is that we tend to get in our own way by recognizing problems, but not focusing on solutions. Over time those problems begin to haunt us, keep negative thoughts flowing through our minds, and we lack the feeling of waking up at peace. We allow the stress and anxiety to negatively impact our daily interactions. We are not taking time to prepare. Goal setting can assist you with these *Peace Disruptors*.

Throughout our lives, we will set many goals. Some goals are bigger than others and will take more time to reach. Then there are short term goals that are far easier to reach. If you sit back and think about some of the goals you have set for yourself this year alone, how many have you accomplished? How many of those goals are you still working toward? Now ask yourself how many of those goals you have given up on already?

We are three months into 2021, and I have accomplished some of the goals I listed on my vision board back in January. I still have a few I am focusing on right now that have been more challenging. Do not get discouraged if you feel the need to regroup, refocus, and get back on the train to reaching your goal.

I will give you my steps and ideas on the best ways to approach and accomplish your short-term or long-term goals so that you eliminate some of the negative thoughts and emotions you have running through your minds.

The first step in accomplishing a goal is to create and identify your goal. You want to create a goal that is not only specific, but attainable. Create goals that are important to you, will add value to your life, will make you feel happier, and ultimately feel accomplished. No goal is too big or too small.

I believe creating goals keeps you living, growing, and thriving. Whether you want to lose weight, buy a house, or create a personal goal to become more knowledgeable in a specific area the first step is to identify your goal. I recommend spending some time reflecting on why it is important to you and how it would benefit you. I also recommend you writing your goal down and putting it somewhere visible to you regularly. I post my goals on my dry erase board where I see them each day.

After you have created your goal, now you want to identify what steps you need to take to achieve your goals. It is not enough to say you want to lose weight. You want to be specific in what that process looks like.

Create Peace In Your Life Through Growth & Self-Development

For example:

Goal: I want to lose 30lbs.

Start Date: June 1st

Steps to Reach Goal:

1) I'm going to workout for 45 minutes 4 times a week starting June 1st.

2) I'm going to do 20 minutes of cardio and 25 minutes of weightlifting for each workout.

3) I'm going to give up sodas and sweets until I reach my goal.

4) I'm going to weigh myself every Sunday to track my progress.

By identifying the steps, you need to take to reach your goals, you can stay focused on it and hold yourself accountable.

So now that you have your goal identified and you have listed the steps you need to take to reach your goal, you want to create your timeline. What does your timeline look like? This is the part of the process where you really need to be honest with yourself. Your timeline needs to be realistic and attainable or there is a good chance you will not reach your goal.

For example, it would not be fair to you to set a goal to lose 30lbs in 2 weeks because that would be unrealistic. You would be setting yourself up for failure. This would be a great time to research an accurate amount of time it may take to accomplish your goal, and again, set your timeline so that you can stay on track with it.

At this point you have identified your goal, you have listed the steps to reach your goal, and you have established your timeline for completion. You are making huge progress! Now it is time to hit the ground running and start pursuing your goal! When we set goals, we are initially excited at the thought of the outcome. Our adrenaline is rushing, and we are highly motivated. The key is to continue that same energy throughout the process. Make a deliberate effort to continue pursing your goal until completion.

If you need an accountability partner or need to join groups or organizations that share similar interests in your goal that would be beneficial as well. Sometimes we fall off track or back pedal a bit, but it is up to you to continue to push through until the end. Do not give up on your goal or yourself.

If you follow the steps mentioned you should be at the point of accomplishing your goal. You will feel good, you will feel proud, and most importantly you will feel accomplished. Accomplishments add a certain level of joy, growth, and happiness into our lives. You are never too old or too young to start setting goals and living your best life. I encourage you to set goals, hit your targets, and grow into the best version of yourself by taking it one step at a time.

For as long as I could remember, I have always wanted to own a small business. I had regretted not pursuing entrepreneurship after working with the same company for 10 years. I regretted not giving myself any other opportunities after graduating from college. Ten years went by and I wanted more. I finally decided to pursue my passion and go for what I desired. I took care of my licensing for my business, purchased inventory, created a website, and pretty much had everything I needed to get the ball rolling.

I was able to run my small business successfully for 4 years, but due to unfortunate circumstances, I shuffled my way back into corporate America. I went back to the same company I worked for previously and continued running my small business simultaneously until my passion for leadership outweighed my passion for my business.

Throughout my entrepreneurship journey, I remember loving what I did, loving creating, but the anxiety and worry was overwhelming. This was my only income at the time. I went from the stability of receiving a check every two weeks, to being the sole reason for whether I would have income each week. I was the owner, website designer, marketing team, advertising team, inventory manager, product designer, telemarketer, event employee, and so many more hats fell under my responsibilities. I learned and did it all!

I was not prepared for all the work it would take to create a small business from scratch, but I was able to adapt and learn on the fly. If I were better prepared financially before starting my business, I believe that the anxiety and worry about my finances at the time would have decreased drastically. A silver lining through this experience was when I re-entered corporate America, the experience and knowledge I gained over those 4 years propelled me into promotions quickly.

My initial *Peace Disruptor* was regret. Then after pursuing my passion, it shifted to anxiety and worry. In both chapters of my life, preparation by goal setting would have been the best solution.

One thing about me is that I adapt to change and life situations well. I am mentally prepared to deal with them because I understand that they are inevitable. Are you preparing mentally for challenging moments? Are you preparing to deal with them and not break? Here are some ideas on what and what not do to when you face tough moments. I recommend that you mentally prepare for life challenges so that you are still able to maintain a certain level of peace throughout each situation.

What Not To Do:

Let me start with what not to do during your challenging moments because this is the side of the spectrum that lean towards negativity and pessimism.

Do Not beat yourself up! Everyone makes mistakes and your ability to learn from them is what helps you grow.

Do Not make rash decisions in the moment that you do not really believe in. For example, do not quit your job, or partake in activities that are dangerous. Do not engage in interactions that you will regret sooner than later.

Do Not sink in your sorrows day after day watching tv, eating ice cream, and consuming alcohol.

Do Not call that person who is already a negative thinker who will help you feed deeper into your anger, sadness, or frustration because that will have a snowball effect on how you are feeling. The snowball will most likely become a snowman! Solutions need to follow the venting session and most negative people lack solutions.

Do Not give up! This may be the most important "Don't". The fact that you are breathing another day is enough to reassure you that you will survive, and you are much stronger and more able than you believe.

What To Do:

Now here is where the goodies come in! Here is what to do when you need to get out of your funk during those ugly moments.

Do take a moment to reflect on what the issues/concerns are. Write them down on one side of a piece of paper. Then on the other side of that paper write down possible solutions. Nothing makes you feel better quicker than coming up with a plan.

Do vent/speak with your support system. That will look different for each person. This support can come from your friend, family, co-workers, or mentor. Just make sure it is someone that tends to have knowledge in the areas of concern and tends to see the glass half full more than half empty. (Choose your vent audience wisely)

Do acknowledge how much you have accomplished so far. Really. Self-acknowledgement will help you feel unstuck because you will be able to realize that if you made it this far, nothing would stop you.

Do get back to doing what you love to do as soon as you can to snap out of feeling overwhelmed or stressed. For me, it was writing again. Writing this book feels good. Getting back into my groove while listening to some feel good music feels refreshing.

Create Peace In Your Life Through Growth & Self-Development

For you, that may be hitting the gym, walking daily, spending time with your friends or family members again. When you go through those challenging times it is easy to become a recluse.
<u>Do</u> wholeheartedly believe that everything happens for a reason. Whether you are in that situation to grow or maybe redirect to shift you towards new opportunities, the outcome will be the best. It can be hard to view it from that perspective while going through it, but it is important to try to take an optimistic view.

Let's face it, we will experience a ton of challenging moments throughout our lives. How we deal with those moments will determine our personal evolution and expansion during our individual journey's.

Be mindful of your decisions and actions during those challenging moments. I know that I will continue to face tower moments while working in Management so through each obstacle I overcome, I will continue to grow and be able to deal with the upcoming towers in a more effective and efficient way. I hope that you all will utilize some of my tips to get through your moments.

Physical preparation and mental preparation go hand in hand with impacting the amount of peace you have in your life in a positive way.

Create Peace In Your Life Through Growth & Self-Development

Meditate daily. Start by challenging yourself to wake up an extra 30 minutes to an hour early to meditate. Meditation allows you to de-clutter the many thoughts that are running through your mind, as well as helps to improve your concentration. Meditation reduces stress and sets a standard of balance throughout your day. It may be difficult starting out but as time goes by, you will begin to appreciate and enjoy those minutes of silence!

Write a to do list weekly. Creating a list allows you to identify tasks that need to be completed throughout your week. This is a great way to prioritize and really helps with your organizational skills. Another benefit of creating a to do list is that it holds you accountable to your actions while helping you stay motivated. Preparation is key!

I created a Preparation Grid on the next page so that you can identify some *Peace Disruptors* you are experiencing in the areas of preparation. Take some time to get better prepared in dealing with some stressors in your life.

Preparation Grid Example:

Peace Disruptors	Problem Areas	Goals/Solutions
Worry/Stress	Lack of Finances	Create a Snowball Payment Program
Regret	Not pursuing passion	Create a Business Plan
Anger	Not receiving promotion	Identify skills you can develop to better position
Fear	Moving to another state that you desire	Create a detailed plan of necessary steps Establish a timeline

Chapter 6: Gratitude

"I Appreciate My Journey. I Love My Life. I Embrace Change."

~Carrie P.~

Chapter 6: Gratitude

Practicing gratitude is the last area to improve in to create peace in your life, but in my opinion, the most important. Being appreciative of the lessons you learn, the highs and the lows, the strength to persevere, the people you have helped along the way, and the will to continue your journey through many life challenges is enough to be thankful for.

When was the last time you said "Thank You" to someone? When was the last time you gave a gift to someone without asking for something in return? Think about the last challenging experience that you had, and instead of regret and anger, you looked for the silver lining because you were still able to live and breathe another day? Gratitude fills you up, allows you to humble yourself, and view life through an optimistic lens.

Journaling

Journaling is a great way to start walking in gratitude to create more peace in your life. I developed a love for journals when I was a teenager. I believe every girl was given a journal at some point in their younger years. It was like the universe knew that we would benefit from expressing ourselves outward. I have 5 journals in my room right now. I accumulated them at different moments in my life over the last few years. Each journal I have has a powerful, relatable image on the cover that was like a magnetic field that had the ability to draw me to purchase it. Whether I was at a bookstore, attending a lecture, or shopping at a retail store, I have been attracted to journals and find so much value in them.

I love journals because journals allow you to express yourself. When we continuously hold in a variety of emotions and experiences, it holds us down. It prevents us from moving on. It interferes with us being able to move on, for healing. Not everyone has the funds to seek counseling or therapy. And honestly, some of us believe we do not need or will benefit from counseling. One thing you experience from counseling is releasing emotions, pain, and unsettling experiences. Having a journal allows you to release as well, on your terms, at your own time. Writing in a journal allows you to express yourself and release that baggage that is weighing you down.

Journals allow you to be truly honest with yourself. No judgement, no worry of others opinion, just privacy and comfortableness. If you are not honest with yourself, who can you be honest with? The more honest you are with yourself, the more opportunities you create to start the healing process. Being able to acknowledge your mistakes, flaws, areas to improve on, and open feelings will aid you in growth and better future experiences.

Journals have a variety of benefits like having the ability to focus on building self-love and showing self- appreciation as well. It is a great opportunity to highlight your accomplishments, successes, growth, and positive attributes.

One of the coolest parts of utilizing journals is that you can go back and view the state of mind you were in weeks, months, and years ago. You can see how far you have come. You can identify your progressions in life. You can identify areas that you may still need to work on.

I looked in one of my journals from 2009 and I was focused on starting a vending machine business at the time. What is ironic is that I started and ran a Gift Basket and Tu-Tu business in 2014 for 4 years. It felt good to reflect on the fact that I have been wanting to become an entrepreneur for a long time. And not only was it a thought, but I made it happen. I would recommend checking your journal just to see if you were able to grow and accomplish goals you intended to in the past.

Overall, I am a believer in journals. I believe they have value in growing. They have value in self-accountability, developing self-love, and establishing self-appreciation. They aid in healing mentally and emotionally, and they are inexpensive. Walk in your truth, into your peace of mind via pen and paper.

Say Thank You

I always tell my team thank you and express how much I appreciate them. I tell my sons thank you in all their efforts. I want to say thank you for reading my book! Some people tend to think you should not have to say thank you to people who are doing a job they get paid for. Some people believe you should not say thank you to your children for completing tasks that they are responsible for. I say thank you because it not only feels good to me, but to the person receiving those two words.

Gratitude and appreciation can lead to better relationships and warmer hearts. It leads to reduced conflict and better daily interactions. Everyone wants to feel appreciated, and a simple thank you does the job.

Spread Joy

Have you ever experienced a rough morning and a family member or friend called you or sent a text and made you laugh? You felt so good that you had to remind yourself that life is good.

You thought about why you were so uneasy and upset and realized that it was not worth it. The same way people can spread joy to you, make a conscious effort to spread joy to others on a consistent basis.

My first business was *Carrie's Every Moment Gift Baskets*. My motto was *Spreading Joy One Basket At A Time*. I sold over a thousand gift baskets over the course of 4 years, all handmade and created by me. I eventually branched out and created and sold hundreds of tutus for girls, teens, and women as well. The most fulfilling moment of every transaction and interaction was the smile and joy I received from each customer when they saw what I created. That feeling was more powerful than the amount of money I received. I loved creating and I loved bringing smiles to so many lives. I was spreading joy every single day and that filled me with so much gratitude.

I greet each one of my employees with eye contact and a genuine smile each day. I send random I Love You texts to my sons for no reason other than making them smile and to let them know that no matter how old they get they are still truly special.

<u>Say I Love You</u>

Create Peace In Your Life Through Growth & Self-Development

Tell your spouse, children, parents, or friends "I Love You". When you verbally speak those words you smile, a heart-warming thought comes to mind, or you experience a great feeling of joy. Love is the greatest feeling in life. The ability to care, show affection, and resonate emotionally with someone creates happiness.

Love others

Gratitude is loving others even when they are not loving themselves. There are times when some people will take advantage of others at their lowest points in life. They believe that because you do not see the value in you, they should not treat you with respect and high regards.

When you are filled with gratitude, you treat others the way you want to be treated no matter how they feel about themselves. Loving others through their pain and struggles brings a great level of internal satisfaction.

Transform other lives

It takes a special kind of someone to feel enriched as you transform others lives. I am big on perspectives. My intentions are to always see the glass half full and not half empty. Some people like to see the entire glass empty and that brings them comfort. It brings them comfort because if they fail to succeed or pursue things in life that will transform them, they are fine because they already believed that outcome would occur anyway.

The person that transforms lives and gives others a higher and more positive perspective are loaded in gratitude and appreciation for life. I love having conversations with people who are in a negative and complaining space at the start of our conversation. After I let them vent, I give my perspective and it is a game changer. My perspective is in the form of solutions. They may not agree 100% at the time because they are still emotional in the moment, but I have planted the seeds. I gave input that was solution based and hopefully changed their thought process about the situation.

Transforming lives can be as simple as believing in someone when they did not believe in themselves.

Appreciate the highs and the lows

Without the bitter tastes in life how can we genuinely appreciate the sweets? Without the struggles how would we build the stamina and persistence to keep moving along? Without the many challenges we face how would we learn the lessons and ultimately make better decisions in the future?

Create Peace In Your Life Through Growth & Self-Development

The many highs and lows throughout our lives are preparation that helps us grow and be better versions of ourselves. I have not met one person who has only had experiences that were great. I also have not met anyone that has had only negative experiences throughout their life.

With that being said, we are all balancing lovely experiences and challenging experiences. When you begin appreciating the not so good experiences you have, that eases the pressure and expectations you have about your life. It removes some of those *Peace Disruptors* that continuously occur in your mind. After you vent and let out the emotional aspect of a low moment for you, look for the solution and find the lesson in that experience. You will feel so much better afterwards.

Give to others what you consider your gifts

We all have gifts. Let me repeat that for you. WE ALL HAVE GIFTS. The moment you realize your gifts and begin sharing them with others you will be filled with gratitude. The many gifts you have can occur at various moments in your lives.

Michael Jordan's gift was being an amazing basketball player who inspired so many children across the world. Les Brown's gift is to motivate and inspire so many people across the world via motivational speaking. Rosalind Brewer is the only black women to lead a Fortune 500 company from the same company I work for: *Walgreens*. She has motivated and inspired so many women in leadership. Jay Shetty has shared his journey of being a Monk and has inspired millions to live in their purpose.

Your level of inspiration can be big or small, but you first need to realize that you have gifts to offer the world. Once you identify your gifts you will become a great inspiration to others and begin walking in shoes filled with gratitude.

Create a List of What You are Grateful For

We are constantly moving at a fast pace in this day in age, and we may not find the time to identify the great things that are happening in our lives.

We sometimes allow stress to cloud our view on what we should be grateful for. I recommend creating a list of affirmations as reminders of the aspects of our lives that bring us so much value and love. If you post these affirmations somewhere visible to you each day, they will increase not only your gratitude in life, but a certain level of peace in your life as well.

Create Peace In Your Life Through Growth & Self-Development

Example Affirmations:

I Am grateful for my family.

I Am grateful for life.

I Am grateful for happiness.

I Am grateful for peace.

I Am grateful for clarity.

I Am grateful for love.

I Am grateful for good health.

I Am grateful for my career.

I Am grateful for abundance.

I Am grateful for the ability to pursue my goals.

I Am grateful for my ancestors.

I Am grateful for continuous learning.

I Am grateful for life skills development.

I Am grateful for my patience.

I Am grateful for joy.

I Am grateful for encouragement.

I Am grateful for friendship and relationships.

I Am grateful for integrity.

I Am grateful for being in tune with my spirit.

I Am grateful for understanding.

I Am grateful for mental strength.

I Am grateful for my success.

I Am grateful for my needs being met.

I Am grateful for my visions.

Conclusion

Am I naive in believing that life can be simpler than we make it? That we can recover from past traumas by changing our perspectives on the situations that have occurred in our lives? That the more self-love we develop, the happier we become overall? Maybe...but Maybe not

We all go through periods in life where we feel hurt, pain, loneliness, regret, anger, bitterness, loss, brokenness, and disappointment. Through those tough periods you were enough.

You can only love from your level and understanding of what love is. You can only behave in manners that you understand to be normal behaviors. You can only make decisions that you believe to be logical in that period of your life. You can only control your responses and outlooks on situations that occurred.

We experience people in different phases of life and there are always learning curves involved in those relationships. When you realize that you cannot control anyone outside of you and how you respond to those experiences, you can recover more easily from any negative experiences attached to that situation.

Create Peace In Your Life Through Growth & Self-Development

The key to repairing the hurt, damage, and negative thoughts from those encounters and circumstances is realizing that **<u>YOU ARE ENOUGH</u>**.

You are enough. You are deserving of love and happiness. Do not harbor and wallow into the abyss of feeling that you are not worthy and deserving to experience a fruitful life. That negative experience you had was the Creator's way of deterring your life in a different direction. There is no road map to this thing we call *Life*. It is not black and white. When you realize that you are enough, you make better decisions, value relationships, and begin to live life on your terms.

There is always room for improvements, but I make a conscious effort to be a better woman each day I can breathe fresh air, while reminding myself that I am enough, and I deserve to live a peaceful life. You deserve a peaceful life as well!

I passionately believe that if you focus on the six areas that I discussed in this book, you will begin to develop peace in your life.

~Practice Self-Care habits and activities. Be a priority in your life.

~Develop Self- Love in everything that you do. You are special.

~Do not run from Self-Accountability. This is mental freedom for you.

~Be considerate and learn to Communicate Effectively. Instead of being over emotional, think logically and practice critical thinking.

~Preparation is crucial for a more consistent life. Practice goal setting.

~By walking in Gratitude, you will become more appreciative of each experience you face in life from an optimistic perspective.

I hope this book has given you varying perspectives on how to create peace in your life through growth and self-development. I am sending you all an abundance of positive and healing energy. Enjoy your journey.

Sending you all Love, Peace, and Light. ~Carrie P.~

Acknowledgments

~Thank you to my Sun's Colin and Caleb. I Love you both so much. You continue to impact my growth more than you know.

~Thank you to my Mom and siblings (Evan and Freddy). The road has not always been easy for us, but we continue to learn and grow each day. Thank you for your support. Love you all.

~Thank you to my cousin Blair for always being one of my biggest supporters in life. Love you dearly.

~Thank you to my ancestors for moving through me and guiding me to be a better example of your legacies.

~Thank you to Risi for giving me the idea and inspiration for this book. I deeply appreciate you.

~Thank you to the many Managers that I have encountered over the last 16 years who have given me various ideas of what a great leader should reflect.

~Thank you to my family and friends near and far who have been supportive in a variety of ways throughout my life. Your mental, emotional, and physical support has helped me grow into who I am becoming.

About the Author

Carrie Porter is a Mother, Author, Manager, Entrepreneur, Blogger, and true Optimist. She has a Bachelor's Degree in Business Administration, and a Master's of Management Degree as well. Carrie was a teen Mom who remained self-motivated to meet goals and obtain accomplishments throughout her life. She believes that there is always a silver lining, growth aspect, and lesson to be learned in every obstacle we encounter.

Carrie is a Vegetarian who loves live Jazz, Shark Tank, and enjoys being out in nature. She desires to motivate, inspire, and encourage others to live a life filled with joy and true optimism!

Create Peace In Your Life Through Growth & Self-Development

BONUS For The Reader!

List some areas you would like to grow and develop over the next year and the reasons why:

Create Peace In Your Life Through Growth & Self-Development

Now list the *action steps* for each area you selected:

<u>Finally, fill the next two pages with inspirational affirmations that will assist you in self-development on your journey to creating a more Peaceful Life:</u>

The Church of All Worlds

Contemporary Paganism, as it exists today, began with the Counterculture movement of the 1960s and 1970s. Religious studies scholar Sarah Pike dates the origins of contemporary Paganism to 1967, the year that Frederick Adams incorporated Feraferia and the New Reformed Order of the Golden Dawn was founded. That same year, the Church of All Worlds filed for incorporation as the first [self-proclaimed] "Pagan" church. ~ "It's Been 50 Years and What Have Pagans Accomplished?" AllergicPagan.com. 4/12/2017

Robert A. Heinlein's bestselling science fiction novel, *Stranger in a Strange Land* (1961), became the foundational scripture of the Church of All Worlds (CAW), a Gaea-oriented Pagan religion founded in 1962 by two American college students, Tim Zell (b. 1942) and (Richard) Lance Christie (1944-2010) who met at Westminster College, Fulton, Missouri, and became fast friends. CAW is named for the fictional church in Heinlein's novel. Tim Zell, now Oberon Zell, is an influential contemporary Pagan leader, and his church has developed a revolutionary programme for the transformation of Western society. CAW core doctrines ('Thou art God'), rituals (water-sharing), and church organizations (nests) are based on those of Heinlein's fictional church. ~ **Carole Cusack** "Robert A. Heinlein's *Stranger in a Strange Land* and the Church of All Worlds," 2008

Among the largest and most influential of all Neo-Pagan religious groups during the 1970s was the Church of All Worlds (CAW). The Church traces its history back to April 7, 1962, when a "water-brotherhood," called "Atl," was formed by Tim Zell and Lance Christie at Westminster College in Fulton, Missouri. A periodical, *The Atlan Torch* (later *The Atlan Annals*), was published, 1962-1968. In 1968, following a move to St. Louis, Missouri, the Church of All Worlds was legally incorporated. In March of that year, the *Green Egg* appeared. From its inauspicious beginnings as a one-page ditto sheet, it grew into a 60-page journal over the next 80 issues, becoming the most significant periodical in the Pagan movement during the 1970s and made Tim Zell, its editor, a major force in Neo-Paganism (a term which Zell coined). ~ **Rev. J. Gordon Melton** *The Encyclopedia of American Religions,* 1991

CAW helped a large number of distinct groups to realize they shared a common purpose, and this gave the phenomenon new significance. Until then, each group had existed on its own, coming into contact with others only at rare events like the Renaissance fairs in California or science fiction conventions. CAW and Tim Zell, by using terms like *Pagan* and *Neo-Pagan* in referring to the emerging collectivity of new Earth religions, linked these groups, and *Green Egg* created a communications network among them. ~ **Margot Adler,** *Drawing Down the Moon,* 1979

The Church of All Worlds has been one of the three most important and influential expressions of Paganism in America, the others being Pagan Witchcraft and Druidry, and it has been primarily developed and sustained by Oberon Zell and his late partner Morning Glory. ~**Ronald Hutton** *Triumph of the Moon: A History of Modern Pagan Witchcraft,* 2000

The Church of All Worlds (CAW) was founded in the tumultuous 1960s and has flourished, with occasional turbulence, into the twenty-first century. Inspired by *Stranger in a Strange Land* and led by Oberon Zell, the CAW represents the continuing human endeavor to reach for a radiant future amid the circle of life and immanence of spiritual transcendence.

As a uniquely American NeoPagan church with international scope, CAW pioneered the eco-spiritual worldview and restored lost wisdom from the past while obsessing about how to beautify the future. I believe it represents no less than a template for how humanity might, and probably will, craft the coming century into an enduring legacy of peace, prosperity, compassion and love—perennial values that live in the heart like seedlings in the dark soil of evolutionary destiny and abiding hope. ~ **Alder Moonoak** *Radiant Circles: Ecospirituality and the Church of All Worlds,* 2022

Books by Oberon Zell

1. *Occult Crime & Ritual Abuse: Who's Who & What's What* (CAW; 4 editions, 1989-1992)
2. *Grimoire for the Apprentice Wizard,* with the Grey Council (New Page, 2004)
3. *Companion for the Apprentice Wizard,* with the Faculty of the Grey School of Wizardry (New Page, 2006)
4. *Creating Circles & Ceremonies: Rituals for All Seasons & Reasons,* with Morning Glory Zell (New Page, 2006)
5. *A Wizard's Bestiary,* with Ash DeKirk (New Page, 2007)
6. *Green Egg Omelette: An Anthology of Art and Articles from the Legendary Pagan Journal* (New Page, 2008)
7. *Prophecy & the End of the World (as we know it): Apocalypse or Solartopia?* with Harvey Wasserman (Solartopia, 2012)
8. *Barsoom: A New Map of the Mars of Edgar Rice Burroughs' "John Carter of Mars" Novels* (TheaGenesis e-book, 2012)
9. *The Wizard and the Witch: Seven Decades of Counterculture, Magick, and Paganism: An Oral History of Oberon Zell and Morning Glory,* by John C. Sulak with Oberon & Morning Glory Zell (Llewellyn, 2014)
10. *Death Rights & Rites: A Practical Guide to a Meaningful Death,* with Judith Fenley (Llewellyn, 2020)
11. *That Undiscover'd Country: A Traveler's Guide to the Afterlife,* with Phaedra Bonewits (Black Moon Pubs, 2021)
12. *Song of Gaea,* with Kiri Johnson (a children's book) Art by Oberon, Sage Lampros, Pratima Sarkar (TheaGenesis, 2021)
13. *Goodbye Jesus, I've Gone Home to Mother* (Left Hand Press, 2021)
14. *The Wizard and the Witch: Special two-volume expanded edition*, by John C. Sulak with Oberon & Morning Glory Zell (Left Hand Press, 2021)
15. *Barsoom: Mapping the Mythic Mars* (TheaGenesis, 2022)
16. *A Wizard's Bestiary* (2nd Edition), with Ash DeKirk (Left Hand Press, 2022)
17. *GaeaGenesis: Conception and Birth of the Living Earth* (Left Hand Press, 2022)
18. *Hystory's Mysteries: Turning Points that Changed Our World*, with Nicholas Kingsley (Left Hand Press, 2024)
19. *Handbook For Our Future Parents: Raising the Magickal Child*, with Haleigh Isbill (Left Hand Press, 2024)
20. *Sharing Water: Church of All Worlds Member Handbook* (Church of All Worlds, 2024)
21. *Church of All Worlds Clergy Handbook* (Church of All Worlds, 2024)
22. *The Hunting of the Ri,* with Morning Glory Zell, Tom Williams, Daniel Blair-Stewart (Ecosophical Research Association, 2025)

Books in process

A Wizard's Guide to Witchy Women, with Rhiannon Zell
Grimoire for the Apprentice Wizard—special Master Edition (Red Wheel/Weiser)
Grimoire for the Journeyman Wizard (Red Wheel/Weiser)
Legendary Journeys: Europe 1987, with Dona Carter (journal entries and color photos from our travels to sacred sites around the world)
Walkabout of the Wandering Wizard (OZ's Journal 2018-2019)
HAM (How About Magick?) (all the issues of the 1990s Pagan kids' magazine in a single volume)
Wizards of the World, with Nikki "Solaris" Kirby & George Knowles.
Unicorns in Our Garden, with Morning Glory Zell (a beautiful coffee-table book of color photos, news-clippings, and writings about our legendary Living Unicorns of the 1980s)